CAPABILITY BROWN
The Master Gardener

by Peter Brimacombe

PETWORTH

J.M.W. Turner's lyrical painting of Capability Brown's landscaped park at Petworth, viewed from the house – a scene that is little changed today. The painting hangs in the house, together with Turner's A Stag Drinking, *commissioned by the 3rd Lord Egremont, whose father employed Brown. Petworth is now owned by The National Trust.*

The Early Years

LANCELOT BROWN was born in 1716 at Kirkharle, a small Northumberland village near Hadrian's Wall. The story that he was the result of a brief flirtation between a pretty chambermaid and the local squire carries some credibility, as Lancelot is an unusual name for a working-class lad, and he remained at school until he was 16, when he was employed by the squire, Sir William Loraine, in his vegetable garden. Brown had no interest in vegetables – indeed, in the majority of his later designs they were banished to a remote location, and 19th-century visitors to Chatsworth wishing to see the vegetable garden were advised to call a carriage! Nonetheless, Sir William's interest in gardening and developing his estate introduced Brown to his own lifelong passion. He remained at Kirkharle until he was 23 when, armed with an introduction from Lady Loraine, he journeyed south to Oxfordshire and found employment at Wootton, near Blenheim Palace, which was later to become one of his greatest landscaped parks.

Brown grew up at a time of radical change in the nation's gardens. The rigid formality of earlier centuries was softened as elaborate parterres, spectacular fountains and clipped topiary gave way to a more natural look inspired by the landscape paintings of artists such as Claude Lorrain and Salvator Rosa, discovered by the English aristocracy while on the 'Grand Tour' in Europe.

The instigators of this novel approach to garden design were the architects Sir John Vanbrugh and William Kent, together with the designer Charles Bridgeman. These three highly talented individuals developed the renowned gardens at Stowe in Buckinghamshire, and Brown was to discover their pioneering work when he moved there in 1740.

PRE-BROWN GARDEN DESIGN

This painting shows the formal garden design most evident in both England and continental Europe prior to the 18th century. Capability Brown was destined to transform this in a dramatic fashion, introducing 'le style anglais' into the nation's gardens.

KIRKHARLE HALL

An illustration of Kirkharle Hall from Pedigree and Memoirs of the Family of Loraine of Kirkharle, *published by Sir Lampton Loraine in 1902. Here Brown spent seven years learning the basics of horticulture.*

CLAUDE LORRAIN

A painting of the Italian country-side by Claude Lorrain, 1648. Lorrain's work had a profound influence on early 18th-century English garden design. He was foremost in introducing pure landscape painting and, as Alexander Pope stated, 'all gardening is landscape painting.'

TOPIARY

The topiary at Parnham in Dorset is typical of the treatment given to trees and bushes prior to the 18th century, whereafter they were left to grow in their natural shape. Rills or watercourses in turn became gracefully curved and far less formal in appearance.

INVENTION OF THE HA-HA

The ha-ha at Claydon House, near Stowe in Buckinghamshire. Charles Bridgeman is credited with inventing the ha-ha. This ingenious device enabled the garden to be linked to the surrounding landscape without visual barriers, while still affording protection from unwanted invaders.

To Stowe

STOWE REPRESENTED a definitive early landscaped park, and marks the end of the English preoccupation with European garden design, being a visual expression of the philosophical considerations prevailing in England during the first half of the 18th century – the Age of Reason. Bridgeman prepared the original plan in 1713, and Kent developed it from 1730 onwards, creating a series of neo-classical buildings throughout the grounds such as the Temple of British Worthies, the Temple of Ancient Virtue and the Palladian Bridge. Stowe was much visited and greatly admired.

Stowe's owner was Lord Cobham, who had enjoyed a highly successful military career as one of Marlborough's generals and was politically prominent in the Whigs, the main rivals to the Tories. Having quarrelled with the Prime Minister, Sir Robert Walpole, in 1733, Cobham turned all his attention to developing Stowe. Brown was promoted to head gardener, and became closely involved with imple-menting the visionary concepts of Bridgeman and Kent, working alongside the latter until his death in 1748.

These were formative years for Lancelot Brown, greatly influencing his thinking in laying out the great land-scaped parks that would later ensure his lasting reputation. However, Stowe was just the beginning, for Brown was to develop the art of a landscaped park far beyond the concepts of Bridgeman and Kent, into something completely unique.

During these happy, uninter-rupted times, Brown met and married Bridget Wayet, and they lived in one of the pair of pavilions standing alongside Oxford Avenue, Stowe's main drive. Their first chil-dren, Bridget and Lancelot, were born shortly afterwards. When Lord Cobham died, 18 months after Kent, Brown felt it was time for a change, and in the autumn of 1751 he moved his family to Hammersmith on the outskirts of London, where he established his own business. Brown was now 35, and on the edge of greatness.

MARRIAGE TO BRIDGET
The Oxford Bridge at Stowe with, beyond, one of the pair of Boycott Pavilions designed by James Gibbs in about 1728. Brown and his wife Bridget, married in 1744 at St Mary's Church on the estate, lived in the other pavilion while at Stowe.

LORD COBHAM
Lord Cobham's marriage to Anne Halsey, a wealthy heiress, enabled him to fulfil his vision of Stowe as a truly great landscaped garden.

THE TEMPLE OF BRITISH WORTHIES

William Kent's Temple of British Worthies stands beside a lake in the Elysian Fields at Stowe. The busts in the curved screen represent great national heroes including Sir Francis Drake and King Alfred, along with the famous writers Shakespeare, Milton and Pope.

THE PALLADIAN BRIDGE

The Palladian Bridge, standing at the head of a large lake, was also built by William Kent. A number of classical buildings were created to enhance the park, now owned by The National Trust.

PLANNING STOWE

Charles Bridgeman's plan for the gardens at Stowe. While Bridgeman introduced such innovations as the ha-ha, he retained a geometric formality, and it was Kent, assisted by Brown, who developed the park as seen today.

Early Commissions

THE INITIAL independent commissions undertaken by Brown were at Warwick Castle for Lord Brooke, later the 1st Earl of Warwick, and Croome Court in Worcestershire, owned by the 6th Earl of Coventry. Brown began work at Warwick around 1750 on a difficult site sandwiched between the River Avon and the town. When the writer Horace Walpole visited in the summer of 1751 he was much impressed: 'The castle is enchanting, the view pleases me more than I can express … It is very well laid out by one Brown.' Walpole became an enthusiastic champion of Brown's work.

At Croome Court, Brown designed the park and also built a fine Palladian house for the owner, the first indication of his talent for architecture. The Earl was delighted. 'Mr Brown has done very well by me,' he wrote. Lancelot Brown had well and truly arrived, and other major commissions followed. The 2nd Earl of Egremont asked him to lay out the park at Petworth in West Sussex, Lord Anson requested his services at Moor Park in Surrey, and further north Brown began working for the Earl of Exeter at Burghley, in Lincolnshire, a task that was to last a lifetime.

All these landscaped parks displayed Brown's distinctive mark. He had by now developed a readily identifiable formula, greatly appealing to the autocratic English aristocracy of the time who desired to inhabit a private, peaceful, Arcadian world, and could easily afford it.

Brown's maxim was 'a good plan, good execution, a perfect knowledge of the country and the objects in it, whether natural or artificial, hiding what is disagreeable, highlighting what is beautiful'. His simple recipe of smooth turf stretching away from the house, past distinctive clumps of trees to a tranquil lake with distant surrounding tree-belt, was skilfully recycled the length and breadth of the nation.

PORTRAIT OF A MASTER GARDENER

Richard Cosway's perceptive portrait of Capability Brown, painted between 1770 and 1775, conveys an intelligent man with a good sense of humour. Self-assured, and with a quiet dignity, Brown quickly gained the respect of his social superiors.

CROOME COURT

The Palladian mansion and land-scaped park at Croome Court, both created by Lancelot Brown. Croome, Brown's first architectural commission, enabled him to make use of the building knowledge he acquired as Clerk of Works at Stowe under William Kent.

THE ROTUNDA, PETWORTH

The Rotunda at Petworth House in West Sussex is one of a number of classical buildings in the park laid out by Capability Brown for the Earl of Egremont between 1753 and 1761.

WARWICK CASTLE

Canaletto's painting in the Birmingham Museum and Art Gallery portrays the East Front of Warwick Castle from the park, around the time that Brown undertook his first commission there in 1750.

THE PARK AT WARWICK CASTLE

The view from the Peacock Garden at Warwick Castle across the River Avon to Brown's park. Begun in the mid-18th century, it remains magnificently unspoilt some 250 years later, and is a superb example of his genius as a landscape designer.

The Road to Success

BROWN'S SUCCESSFUL career owed as much to a natural ability to get on well with his wealthy aristocratic clients as it did to his technical and artistic talent. Although he came from a humble background, Brown demonstrated a remarkable aptitude to relate to a haughty 18th-century nobility requiring their social inferiors to be suitably deferential, and his confident, knowledgeable attitude ensured a ready acceptance into high society. He became personal friends with many of his clients, dining with them regularly.

Brown's skilful handling of his superiors stood him in good stead when the dissolute 3rd Viscount Weymouth engaged him to lay out the park at Longleat in Wiltshire. The debauched Weymouth drank and gambled until dawn and had a string of creditors, yet Brown maintained an excellent relationship with him, and was paid in full for the job, which took six years to complete. Today, this outstanding example of the English Renaissance stands in a superb setting.

In 1760 Brown began work at Corsham Court in Wiltshire, where he was engaged to alter both the house and the grounds. During the same period he was commissioned by the 4th Duke of Devonshire at Chatsworth in Derbyshire, sweeping away Henry Wise's parterres and what Walpole dismissively described as 'many foolish waterworks', though surprisingly sparing Grillet's Great Cascade together with the Sea Horse Fountain on the South Lawn. This commission involved altering the course of the River Derwent and moving the village of Edensor to establish a new entrance and drive. In an age uninhibited by planning regulations, such changes presented little problem.

Today, much of Brown's work survives as an excellent example of his design both at Chatsworth and at another Midland property, Charlecote, outside Stratford.

CHATSWORTH
A view of Chatsworth, the Derbyshire home of the Duke and Duchess of Devonshire. The three-arched bridge was constructed by James Paine to carry a new drive created by Brown as part of his landscaping for the 4th Duke.

THE PATH TO EDENSOR
The 11th Duchess of Devonshire regrets some of the changes Brown made to the gardens at Chatsworth, yet considers his treatment of the park to be 'peerless'. This view shows the path running across the estate towards the village of Edensor.

CHARLECOTE
A view of the West Front of Charlecote in Warwickshire across the River Avon, showing the park begun by Brown in the early 1750s. It has an extensive ha-ha to keep out the deer.

CORSHAM COURT

Corsham Court is another great Wiltshire estate where Brown laid out the park and also worked on the house. He is believed to have planted the oriental plane tree shown here.

LONGLEAT

This early 19th-century sketch portrays the landscaped park at Longleat in Wiltshire some 60 years after Brown laid it out for the 3rd Viscount Weymouth. Despite the ravages of time and the great storm of 1990, it remains one of Brown's classic creations.

The Best of Brown

IN THE early 1760s Capability Brown, as he had become known, began work on the two magnificent landscaped parks now widely considered to be his greatest masterpieces. He was employed at Bowood in Wiltshire by the 2nd Earl of Shelburne, who later became the Marquis of Lansdowne, and shortly afterwards by the 4th Duke of Marlborough at Blenheim Palace in Oxfordshire. Both men were highly energetic and enterprising, determined to enhance their estates and leave their mark for posterity. The houses were the creations of outstanding English architects – Henry Keene and Robert Adam at Bowood, and the illustrious Sir John Vanbrugh at Blenheim – and were fine buildings calling for appropriately elegant surroundings. 'Capability' was equal to the challenge.

At both places, Brown created huge lakes by damming insignificant streams. The larger of these lakes was at Blenheim, where Brown partially submerged Vanbrugh's rather cumbersome bridge – he was completely uninhibited by anything he found in his way, regardless of the creator's reputation, and had no compunction in removing it. Thus Wise's parterre at Blenheim suffered the same fate as at Chatsworth. Such cultural vandalism proved worthwhile, for when King George III visited Blenheim he was deeply impressed. Gazing across the lake to the bridge and the house beyond, England's monarch exclaimed, 'We have nothing like this.' Lord Randolph Churchill, younger brother of the 8th Duke and father of Sir Winston Churchill, who was born at Blenheim, considered it 'the finest view in England'.

At Bowood, the view from the house down a grassy slope, dotted with characteristic clumps of trees to the lake beyond, is classic Capability Brown. Behind the lake is a small Doric temple on a mound, with a backdrop of tall trees reflected in the calm waters. There is a marvellous air of timeless tranquillity – the English landscape at its pristine best.

BLENHEIM
The view in early evening across the lake at Blenheim, which Brown formed by damming the River Glyme. Vanbrugh's partly submerged Great Bridge is on the left, and Blenheim Palace lies on the hill beyond, bathed in sunlight.

THE 1ST MARQUIS OF LANSDOWNE
Sir Joshua Reynolds' portrait of the 2nd Earl of Shelburne, later created 1st Marquis of Lansdowne by George III. He was an energetic visionary who engaged Robert Adam to extend Bowood, his house in Wiltshire, and commissioned Capability Brown to 'improve' the estate.

BOWOOD
Looking across the lake at Bowood towards the Doric temple, on a calm evening. The present Marquis of Lansdowne comments, 'I would say, without wishing to appear boastful, that this Capability Brown park is one of the most beautiful in the country.' Few would disagree.

THE 4TH DUKE OF MARLBOROUGH
Reynolds' fine portrait of the 4th Duke of Marlborough with his family hangs in the Red Drawing Room at Blenheim. The present Duke declares, 'a visitor entering through the gate from Woodstock today would immediately appreciate Brown's genius.'

Across the Nation

FEW INDIVIDUALS have displayed such a profound and lasting impact on the English countryside or left such an indelible mark right across the nation as Capability Brown. From Alnwick in Northumberland, not far from the Scottish border, to Ugbrooke in deepest Devon, his work is still much in evidence today, nearly two and a half centuries after it was conceived.

Brown's energy appeared boundless, creating more than a hundred landscaped parks – virtually all England's great stately homes nestle in a Capability Brown setting. His output was prodigious, quite remarkable considering the poor communications prevailing in the mid-18th century, and that Brown, a lifelong asthmatic, constantly suffered from poor health. Nevertheless, he shuttled continually around the country by horse-drawn carriage, on roads little better than dirt tracks, to Burghley in Lincolnshire, via Audley End in East Anglia, down to Luton Hoo in Bedford-shire and to Prior Park on the edge of Bath, with the help of only a handful of assistants and a great deal of unskilled labour.

The ubiquitous Brown possessed an uncanny ability to transform a landscape totally. He built hills on hitherto flat ground, created shimmering lakes on previously dry land and, as his impatient noble clients wanted instant maturity and were not prepared to wait for trees to grow, he perfected a tree-moving device that enabled even giant oaks to be uprooted and moved to achieve the desired effect. Brown was bold and imaginative, inventive with new techniques, effortlessly able to satisfy the aristo-cratic vision of Arcadia and make his wealthy clients' dreams come true. Murmurs of approval travelled rapidly around the corridors of power, and Brown numbered five prime ministers and more than a dozen dukes among his impres-sive list of clients. But it was not to end there, for the ambi-tious Brown desired more – a Royal Appointment.

ALNWICK CASTLE
Alnwick Castle still stands boldly amid the Northumberland countryside, much as it would have appeared when Brown completed the park for the 1st Duke towards the end of the 18th century.

UGBROOKE PARK
Ugbrooke Park in Devon, painted by Hendrick de Cort in 1790, some 30 years after Brown began laying out the park for the Hon. Thomas Clifford. Brown is also considered to have built the house, which has a Robert Adam interior.

BURGHLEY HOUSE
A view of Burghley House, seat of the Marquis of Exeter, around 1819, depicting the house beyond the mile-long lake, spanned by the Lion Bridge. Brown worked extensively on both house and grounds throughout the 1760s and 70s.

THE LION BRIDGE
The Lion Bridge at Burghley, framing the house originally built by Lord Burghley, Queen Elizabeth I's powerful Lord High Treasurer. Brown described Burghley as the place 'where I have had 25 years' pleasure, restoring the monument of a great minister to a great Queen'.

AUDLEY END
Brown's plan for Audley End near Cambridge, prepared and executed in the 1760s for Sir John Griffin Griffin, later the 1st Lord Braybrooke. Brown widened the River Cam and planted a considerable number of trees, creating the lovely prospect that remains in evidence today.

The Royal Gardener

AN ANNOUNCEMENT in *The Gentleman's Magazine* in July 1764 confirmed Lancelot Brown as Surveyor to His Majesty's Gardens and Waters at Hampton Court. Brown had coveted the post for a number of years, enlisting some powerful supporters. In 1757 a petition signed by more than a dozen peers was submitted to the Patronage Secretary, the Duke of Newcastle, but it was to be a further seven years, when George III had come to the throne, before Brown acquired the position he so desired. Among his responsibilities was Richmond Park, and shortly after-wards St James's Park was added. In addition to a handsome salary, the position included a late 17th-century residence in the grounds of Hampton Court – Wilderness House, which still stands close to the Lion's Gate.

Surprisingly, Brown made no dramatic changes at Hampton Court, 'out of respect to myself and my profession', despite the urging of the King. When George learnt of Brown's death in 1783, he gleefully told his under-gardener, 'Brown is dead, now you and I can do here as we please.' Brown did, however, plant the Great Vine, which still produces a copious crop of black Hamburg grapes.

Brown instigated a substantial amount of change at Richmond Park, sweeping away formality and cheer-fully eliminating all traces of Bridgeman and Kent, his erstwhile mentors at Stowe. King George was extremely pleased with what he saw.

The architect Sir William Chambers, who had laid out Kew Gardens adjacent to Richmond, including the celebrated Pagoda, held views diametrically opposed to those of Brown, and when the flamboyant Lord Clive of India chose Brown instead of Chambers to create a new house at Claremont in Surrey, a furious Chambers wrote a book on garden design, violently attacking Brown. Brown was deeply shocked, but Chambers' criticism failed to harm his glittering reputation.

KING GEORGE III
King George III's passion for the country-side extended to gardening, and he took a keen personal interest in the major new gardens being developed across his kingdom. He was affectionately known as 'Farmer George'.

THE GREAT VINE AT HAMPTON COURT
Capability Brown planted the Great Vine at Hampton Court Palace. The scale of the figure standing at the far end conveys the gigantic size the vine has now reached, more than 200 years later.

KEW GARDENS

Kew Gardens was designed by Sir William Chambers, who was greatly influenced by the Orient. Although King George was said to be infatuated with the Chinese Pagoda at Kew, he was apparently far more interested in Brown's work at nearby Richmond Park, to Chambers' annoyance.

WILDERNESS HOUSE

Wilderness House at Hampton Court became Brown's residence when he was appointed Surveyor to His Majesty's Gardens and Waters in 1764.

HAMPTON COURT PRIVY GARDENS

The Privy Gardens at Hampton Court, where Brown replaced the terrace steps with gravel and grass slopes. According to Law's History of Hampton Court Palace, *published in 1891, this was 'because we ought not to go up and down stairs in the open air'.*

Just Rewards

AS CAPABILITY Brown's career continued to prosper, he began to enjoy the fruits of success. Substantial fees earned from commissions enabled Brown to send his eldest son, Lancelot, to Eton, where his nickname was 'Capey'. He later became a barrister and entered politics, assisted by his father's powerful circle of aristocratic friends. Brown's younger son, John, enlisted in the Royal Navy, fought in the American War of Independence, and was eventually promoted to Admiral of the Fleet, a career also considerably aided by his father's influential acquaintances.

In 1767 Brown succeeded in purchasing Fenstanton Manor from an impecunious client, the 9th Earl of Northampton, who had encountered severe financial difficulties as a result of excessive gambling and the massive political bribery that was such a feature of election campaigns in those days. The former village lad had now become Lord of the Manor.

Fenstanton was only a few miles north of Cambridge, and Brown quickly became acquainted with the University dons. In 1779 he put forward a grandiose scheme to transform the beautiful area between the colleges and the River Cam, known as the Backs, into one of his archetypal landscaped parks. Brown was, however, to encounter one of the few set-backs of his entire career when the dons steadfastly refused to have the course of the river altered and their individual private college gardens completely obliterated. The rejected plan now lies in the University library, and only at St John's College was Brown able to make his mark at Cambridge.

Fenstanton was in Huntingdonshire, and in 1770 Brown was honoured by being created High Sheriff of the County. Capability Brown had now become a country gentleman; he had acquired both fame and fortune, together with an acknowledged place in 18th-century English high society.

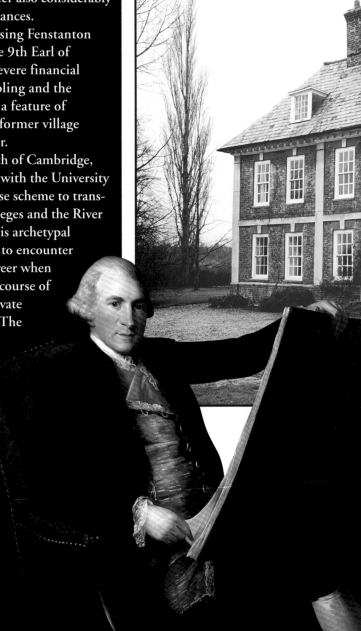

FENSTANTON MANOR
Brown purchased Fenstanton Manor, a small gabled manor house standing close to the road, as his country residence. A plaque on the wall records a fire policy number 551360 purchased by Brown from Sun Insurance in October 1773.

LORD CHATHAM

Brown's close friend and admirer, Lord Chatham, wrote of him: 'He shares the private hours of the King, dines familiarly with his neighbour of Syon [the Duke of Northumberland] and sits down at the tables of all the House of Lords.'

ST JOHN'S COLLEGE, CAMBRIDGE

St John's College, Cambridge, viewed across the Backs with the slow-flowing River Cam in the foreground. In addition to his fee, the grateful Fellows gave Brown a piece of silver plate for his work on the College gardens.

ROBERT ADAM

Robert Adam, undoubtedly the most successful architect of his day, worked alongside Capability Brown on a number of undertakings at places such as Alnwick, Bowood, Syon and Ugbrooke. Their abilities complemented each other to an extraordinary degree.

The Latter Years

WHEN CAPABILITY Brown first moved to Hammersmith in 1751, he met Henry Holland, a builder who lived in nearby Fulham, and thus began a long-lasting friendship and business relationship. Holland's son, also named Henry, became an architect, and married Brown's daughter Bridget in 1773. Brown took his son-in-law into partnership, and they worked together on projects such as Claremont for Lord Clive, and Broadlands, the Hampshire estate of the first Lord Palmerston. In the 20th century, Broadlands was to become the home of Lord Louis Mountbatten, the illustrious Second World War commander and godfather of H.R.H Prince Charles. Brown and Holland transformed the former Jacobean mansion house into the stylish Palladian mansion that can be seen today, while Brown created the gardens which gently slope down to the slow-moving River Test, brilliantly exploiting the potential of the superb location and conceiving a masterpiece which survives into the 21st century.

Brown also produced plans for the 1st Earl of Carnarvon at Highclere in Berkshire during the latter part of the 18th century, worked alongside Robert Adam at Syon in Middlesex on behalf of the Duke of Northumberland, created the exquisite lakes at Sheffield Park in Sussex and fashioned what is widely considered to be his great northern masterpiece, Harewood in Yorkshire, where once again Robert Adam was the architect. In 1798 the painter J.M.W. Turner immortalised a view of Harewood which 200 years later remains essentially the same, encapsulating Brown's meticulous planning and faultless execution. 'True art is nature to advantage dressed,' declared the poet Alexander Pope, words that are well illustrated at Broadlands and Harewood, created at a time when Capability Brown was at his peak. During this period, Brown declined an invitation from the Duke of Leinster to improve his Irish estate 'as I have not yet finished England'.

BROADLANDS

Brown worked on both the house and grounds at Broadlands in Hampshire. He completed the project in 1779, although his son-in-law, Henry Holland, later undertook alterations. Broadlands maintains many of the characteristics that Brown originally bestowed upon it.

SHEFFIELD PARK

In the late 1770s, Brown initiated the construction of a quartet of lakes at Sheffield Park for John Baker, later 1st Earl of Sheffield. The work was completed by Humphrey Repton. In the winter of 1890, the 3rd Earl arranged cricket matches on one of the frozen lakes.

HAREWOOD HOUSE

This view of Harewood, seen alongside J.M.W. Turner's painting of 1798, shows how well Brown's park has been conserved. Sir Charles Barry removed the imposing portico on the South Front when he installed the terrace in the mid-19th century.

SYON PARK

This mid 18th-century engraving depicts Syon across the River Thames from Kew, a view that can still be enjoyed today. Brown worked on the grounds for the Duke of Northumberland, while Robert Adam remodelled the house. Their work was completed in 1773.

HIGHCLERE CASTLE

In 1770 Brown was approached to give the grounds of Highclere Castle a more fashionable, natural look. When Benjamin Disraeli, the famous Prime Minister, first visited Highclere almost a hundred years later, he exclaimed 'How scenical! How scenical!'

Brown's Legacy

ON 6 FEBRUARY 1783, having dined with his old friend Lord Coventry, Brown suffered a massive heart attack outside his daughter's house and died shortly afterwards. He was 67. 'Lady Nature's second husband is dead,' lamented Horace Walpole. Brown died at the height of his powers, with his reputation intact. Subsequently, critics considered his work to lack texture, colour contrast or visual excitement, regarding his style as too bland and repetitive. Yet Brown was a man of vision, and ultimately his unrivalled standing as a gardener has survived the test of time and changing tastes, so that the places he once created to indulge the pampered, privileged few now convey enormous pleasure to the countless thousands visiting the parks he designed so long ago.

His mantle as a landscape gardener was adopted by Humphrey Repton, who embellished Brown's work at places such as Longleat, Corsham and Sheffield Park. Repton was not such a purist as Brown, not averse to terracing and flights of steps, which began to reappear at houses like Harewood and Bowood. Brown's excessive zeal in grassing over the Great Court and removing parterres at Blenheim Palace has been rectified, yet all around the kingdom his powerful presence remains. Capability Brown was more than merely an outstanding gardener – he thought on a grand scale, and joins Christopher Wren and Isambard Brunel as someone who has forever altered the English landscape.

HORACE WALPOLE

Horace Walpole, the 4th Earl of Orford, was the son of Robert Walpole, England's first Prime Minister. Horace Walpole transformed his house at Strawberry Hill in Twickenham into a Gothic castle, and became a self-styled arbiter of good taste.

BLENHEIM PALACE

Capability Brown's huge lake at Blenheim, viewed from the grassy slope running down from the palace. Sir John Vanbrugh's Grand Bridge is in the background beyond a giant copper beech tree, planted by Brown almost 250 years ago.

CLAREMONT

Claremont in Surrey was the property of Lord Clive of India, who commissioned Brown to pull down the house originally built by Sir John Vanbrugh in order to create a splendid new Palladian mansion.

IN MEMORIAM

In the church of Fenstanton where Brown is buried is a memorial to him and his two sons. Horace Walpole wrote: 'Brown shall enjoy unsullied fame for many a paradise regained.'

Acknowledgements

The author would like to thank the Duke and Duchess of Marlborough, the Marquis of Lansdowne, and Katie Fretwell at The National Trust, together with the administrative staff at Harewood, Warwick Castle, Highclere Castle and Croome Court, for their help in the preparation of this guide.

Written by Peter Brimacombe. The author has asserted his moral rights to be recognised as the author of this work.
Edited by Jenni Davis.
Designed by Anne Sharples.
Picture research by Christine Crawshaw.
Front cover designed by John Buckley.
Map by The Map Studio, Romsey, Hants.

Photographs are reproduced with the permission of the following:
John Bethell: 5 inset, 21 inset bottom; The Trustees of the Bowood Collection: 10b; Bridgeman Art Library: front cover right (Private Collection), inside front cover (Petworth House, Sussex), 2–3 (Yale Center for British Art, Paul Mellon Collection), 3tr (Hermitage, St. Petersburg, Russia), 6b (Private Collection), 7c (Birmingham Museums and Art Gallery), 9tl, 9tr (Stapleton Collection), 13t (Private Collection), 14r (Hampton Court Palace), 20 inset (City of Westminster Archive Centre); Peter Brimacombe: front cover bottom left, 3c, 3b, 5t, 5b, 10–11, 11 inset top, 15t, 15c, 17b, 19b, 20–21, back cover top left; The Clifford Estate (Chattels) Ltd.: 12b; Croome Estate Trust: 6–7t; English Heritage: 13 inset; English Life Publications Ltd.: 13b (Newbery Smith Photography); Mary Evans Picture Library: 18t; Fotomas Index: 21 inset top; Reproduced by kind permission of the Earl and Countess of Harewood and Trustees of the Harewood House Trust: 19t, 19cl; Reproduced by kind permission of His Grace the Duke of Marlborough: 11 inset bottom; National Monuments Record: 16–17; National Portrait Gallery: 14 inset, 16b, 17t; National Trust Photographic Library: front cover centre left (Oliver Ben), 4t (John Miller), 7tr, back cover bottom left (Rupert Truman), 8–9b (Matthew Antrobus), 18b (David Sellman); Collection of the Duke of Northumberland: 19cr; Pitkin Unichrome: front cover top left, 15b (A. G. Whitworth); Stowe School Photographic Archives: 4b; David Tarn: 8t, 9cl, 12t, back cover centre left and top right; Audio Visual Centre, University of Newcastle: 2b; Warwick Castle, Warwick, England: 6–7b (John Wright Photography).

Publication in this form © Pitkin Unichrome Ltd 2001.
No part of this publication may be reproduced by any means without the permission of Pitkin Unichrome Ltd and the copyright holders.

Printed in Great Britain.
ISBN 1 84165 039 0   1/01

FS 32611
Pitkin Unichrome is a publishing, design and photographic company registered to ISO 9001 by the British Standards Institution.

SCOTLAND

Legend

ENGLAND

Alnwick

Kirkharle

Newcastle

Durham

Aske Hall

Harewood

York

Leeds

Temple Newsam House

Chatsworth

Derby

Weston Park

Chillington Hall

Birmingham

Burghley

Peterborough

Norwich

Berrington Hall

Coombe Abbey

Ragley Hall

Warwick Castle

Warwick

Charlecote

Fenstanton

St John's College

Cambridge

Wimpole Hall

Euston Hall

Worcester

Castle Ashby

WALES

Moccas Court

Croome Court

Gloucester

Wootton

Stowe

Milton Keynes

Audley End

Blenheim

Oxford

Badminton

Corsham Court

Bath

Bowood

Prior Park

Highclere

Syon Park

Hampton Court

Basingstoke

LONDON

Kew Gardens

Claremont

Maidstone

Leeds Castle

Longleat

Sherborne Castle

Broadlands

Southampton

Winchester

Horsham

Petworth

Sheffield Park

Exeter

Ugbrooke Park

ENGLISH CHANNEL

PITKIN

ISBN 1-84165-039-0

9 781841 650395